Welcome

This little journal is your chance to spend a few minutes with yourself before the day gets away from you.

No rules.
No pressure.

No one is going to see it but you, and you're definitely not getting a grade. Write whatever comes to mind—there's no right or wrong answer, only what's true for you in the moment.

Can I be honest with you? When I first learned about journaling and gratitude practice, I thought it was a bunch of nonsense. I couldn't understand how answering the same questions daily would have any impact on my life. I thought it was a gimmick. I mean, isn't it obvious what I'm grateful for? My family, my dog, my home, my job, etc... How would repeating these things day after day make any difference?

What's more, I didn't want to add something else to my morning routine. It would mean getting up earlier or giving up something like eating breakfast or drying my hair. Ridiculous! I wasn't buying it.

That is...until I was left with no choice. A friend of mine sent me an unexpected gift.

Yep, you guessed it—a gratitude journal. Now what was I going to do?

It was such a thoughtful surprise, I had to at least give it a try.

So, I started setting my morning alarm ten minutes earlier to give myself time to answer the prompts. For the first couple of weeks, my answers were the same every single day. This experiment was proving my theory that it was a waste of time at first, but one morning, something surprising happened.

I was walking my dog, like I did every morning. When I looked up from my phone, the sky was this gorgeous, bright blue. It was so beautiful, I actually stopped and noticed it. I'd walked that same route a hundred times before and never paid much attention. But that morning, I felt genuinely grateful for it— this simple, serene moment right in front of me.

The next day, something shifted. I started picking up on other little things—the leaves rustling in the breeze, the quick but pleasant conversation I had with the woman at the pharmacy, and even how happy it made me to fill up my big pink water jug in the morning.

That's when it clicked:

Gratitude isn't about writing down the same obvious things over and over—it's about opening your eyes to what's already around you, even the little stuff you might usually miss.

My hope is that this journal does the same for you. I hope it helps you slow down, appreciate the little moments, and realize that even on the hard days, there's always something worth noticing...and worth being grateful for.

Why I Created This Journal

Once I truly understood how powerful a simple daily gratitude practice could be, creating this journal felt like the obvious next step. I've written books, workbooks, and **The Sprinkle Effect™ Card Deck**—all designed to help you make small shifts that lead to big change. But if I'm being honest, keeping a gratitude journal has been one of the most instrumental parts of my own growth and transformation over the past decade. So, I hope this journal becomes a simple, meaningful way to start your mornings with gratitude, intention, and a fresh perspective.

Author • Coach • Speaker

 @debbie.r.weiss   ✉ debbie@debbierweiss.com

 @debbierweiss   🌐 www.debbierweiss.com

How to Use This Journal

A Sprinkle of Gratitude provides you with five simple prompts to start your morning with gratitude, intention, and a positive mindset. You'll also be prompted to write a Sprinkle Reflection each day, using your daily theme inspired by **The Sprinkle Effect™**.

If You Have The Sprinkle Effect™ Card Deck:

1. Pick Your Sprinkle: Shuffle the deck or choose one that matches how you're feeling today.

2. Read Your Card: Read the quote, affirmation, and journal prompt.

3. Write the Affirmation: Write the affirmation in the "Sprinkle Affirmation" section in your journal.

4. Answer the Sprinkle Prompt: Use the card's journal prompt to explore your thoughts for the day.

If You Don't Have the Deck (Yet!):

1. **Use the Sprinkle List** on the next page.
2. **Pick a Sprinkle** that speaks to you.
3. **Write** your sprinkle affirmation in your journal.
4. **Reflect:** Write about how you want to embody that sprinkle today.

Your 5 Daily Prompts

1. Today I am grateful for:

Write at least one thing—big or small—that you appreciate right now. It could have happened yesterday or this morning. It could be your health, a kind word, or the first sip of tea. The more specific, the better.

2. My intention for today is:

This is how you want to show up today. It could be "to stay calm in stressful moments," "to listen more than I speak," or "to make progress on my big project." Think of it as your anchor for the day.

3. A challenge I might face today and how I will approach it:

This helps you think ahead and decide in advance how you'll respond instead of react. Maybe you have a tough meeting, a busy schedule, or a difficult conversation ahead—write how you plan to handle it.

4. One thought or belief I'm letting go of today is:

Use this to release something that doesn't serve you. This could be self-doubt, worrying about what others think, or the belief that you have to do everything perfectly. Let it go on paper so it's not weighing you down all day.

5. One thing I will do today to bring joy into my life is:

Joy doesn't have to be big or time-consuming. It could be calling a friend, sitting in the sun for five minutes, dancing to a favorite song, or reading a chapter of a book. Make this something you actually look forward to.

Sprinkle Reflection:

After completing the five prompts, take a minute to connect with your sprinkle of the day. Write the affirmation (if you haven't already done so) and respond to the journal prompt. This ties your gratitude practice to a bigger theme—like resilience, courage, or curiosity—and opens your awareness to how it manifests in unexpected ways.

Sprinkle List

Quote / Affirmation / Journal Prompt

1. Possibilities
"The most exhilarating part of life isn't knowing all the answers; it's discovering who you are and what you're capable of."

I give myself permission to imagine something new and exciting.

What is one thing I've been too nervous to pursue, and what is a small, exciting way to start?

2. Perspective
"Our beliefs, values, and experiences shape the lens through which we see life."

Changing how I look at things can make all the difference.

What's one situation I could see differently? How might that change the way I feel about it?

3. Mindset
"Every challenge is a chance to learn and grow."

I have the power to change my mindset and change my life.

If I really tapped into my positivity today, how could it make a difference for me or the people around me?

4. Belief

"The excuses we tell ourselves are just limiting beliefs. They hold us back from doing what we are truly capable of."

I trust in my ability to create the life I desire.

Which belief, if I strengthened it, could help me get closer to my goals?

5. Courage

"You have everything it takes to face your fears. Every time you show up, take a step, or try again, you are already doing it."

I am braver than I give myself credit for.

What is one fear holding me back, and what is the easiest step I can take to push past it?

6. Responsibility

"I have always had the power to change my life—one response at a time."

By taking responsibility for today, I create the future I want.

"Who or what am I blaming right now, and how can I take responsibility instead?

7. Dreams

"If you don't believe it is possible, then it's not."

Every day, I take a step closer to living my dreams.

If I could dream without limits, what would my life look like a year from now?

8. Direction

"Your dreams are not just fantasies; they're a roadmap to your future."

I don't have to know the whole plan—I just need to take the next step.

Where am I headed right now? Is that where I truly want to go?

9. Vision

"Visualization is about seeing yourself doing the thing you want to accomplish—step by step, with purpose and intention."

I can see it, I can feel it, and I know it's possible.

If I were living my vision today, what would I be doing differently?

10. Action

"Without action, everything that came before is just a dream and a plan."

I take small steps today that lead to big changes tomorrow.

How can I create momentum today, even if I don't feel ready?

11. Discipline

"Discipline isn't about toughing it out—it's about building the life you truly want."

I'm proud of the effort I put in, even when it's hard.

What's one small habit I can stick to today, even if it's tough?

12. Adaptability

"Don't get discouraged by setbacks—use them as stepping stones to grow and learn."

I trust my ability to handle whatever life throws my way.

When was the last time I adapted to a tough situation successfully? What did I learn from it?

13. Resilience

"You are capable of more than you think. Every challenge you overcome helps you not just survive, but thrive."

Every challenge I face makes me stronger.

When I feel like giving up, what helps me keep going?

14. Curiosity

"Curiosity creates new opportunities, making life richer and more interesting."

Every question I ask opens the door to new possibilities.

What is one thing I've always wondered about, and how can I take a step toward learning more?

15. Connection

"The right community—one that shares your values and supports your growth—can change your life."

I choose to surround myself with people who lift me up and bring out the best in me.

What is one way I can strengthen a connection that's important to me?

16. Joy

"Start your day with gratitude. Think of three things you're thankful for before your feet hit the floor."

Today, I'll notice and appreciate the simple things that make me happy.

What has brought me a sense of joy recently, and how can I create more moments like that?

17. New Beginnings

"Your journey is just beginning. You have the power to create a vibrant, extraordinary life—one sprinkle at a time."

Every day is a fresh start and I have the power to create the life I want.

What is one small step I can take toward creating the life I truly want?

Day: _____ Date: _____

Sprinkle of the Day: _____

Sprinkle Affirmation: _____

_____

_____

1. Today I am grateful for: _____

_____

_____

2. My intention for today is: _____

_____

_____

3. A challenge I might face today and how I will approach it:

_____

_____

4. One thought or belief I'm letting go of today is:

_____

_____

5. One thing I will do today to bring joy into my life is:

_____

_____

Sprinkle Reflection:

_____

_____

_____

_____

_____

_____

_____

_____

_____

_____

_____

_____

_____

_____

_____

_____

_____

_____

_____

_____

Day: _____ Date: _____

Sprinkle of the Day: _____

Sprinkle Affirmation: _____

_____

_____

1. Today I am grateful for: _____

_____

_____

2. My intention for today is: _____

_____

_____

3. A challenge I might face today and how I will approach it:

_____

_____

4. One thought or belief I'm letting go of today is:

_____

_____

5. One thing I will do today to bring joy into my life is:

_____

_____

Sprinkle Reflection:

_____

_____

_____

_____

_____

_____

_____

_____

_____

_____

_____

_____

_____

_____

_____

_____

_____

_____

Day: _____ Date: _____

Sprinkle of the Day: _____

Sprinkle Affirmation: _____

_____

_____

1. Today I am grateful for: _____

_____

_____

2. My intention for today is: _____

_____

_____

3. A challenge I might face today and how I will approach it:

_____

_____

4. One thought or belief I'm letting go of today is:

_____

_____

5. One thing I will do today to bring joy into my life is:

_____

_____

Sprinkle Reflection:

_____

_____

_____

_____

_____

_____

_____

_____

_____

_____

_____

_____

_____

_____

_____

_____

_____

_____

_____

_____

_____

Day: _____ Date: _____

Sprinkle of the Day: _____

Sprinkle Affirmation: _____

_____

_____

1. Today I am grateful for: _____

_____

_____

2. My intention for today is: _____

_____

_____

3. A challenge I might face today and how I will approach it:

_____

_____

4. One thought or belief I'm letting go of today is:

_____

_____

5. One thing I will do today to bring joy into my life is:

_____

_____

Sprinkle Reflection:

_____

_____

_____

_____

_____

_____

_____

_____

_____

_____

_____

_____

_____

_____

_____

_____

_____

_____

_____

_____

Day: _____ Date: _____

Sprinkle of the Day: _____

Sprinkle Affirmation: _____

_____

_____

1. Today I am grateful for: _____

_____

_____

2. My intention for today is: _____

_____

_____

3. A challenge I might face today and how I will approach it:

_____

_____

4. One thought or belief I'm letting go of today is:

_____

_____

5. One thing I will do today to bring joy into my life is:

_____

_____

Sprinkle Reflection:

_____

_____

_____

_____

_____

_____

_____

_____

_____

_____

_____

_____

_____

_____

_____

_____

_____

_____

_____

Day: _____ Date: _____

Sprinkle of the Day: _____

Sprinkle Affirmation: _____

_____

_____

1. Today I am grateful for: _____

_____

_____

2. My intention for today is: _____

_____

_____

3. A challenge I might face today and how I will approach it:

_____

_____

4. One thought or belief I'm letting go of today is:

_____

_____

5. One thing I will do today to bring joy into my life is:

_____

_____

Sprinkle Reflection:

_____

_____

_____

_____

_____

_____

_____

_____

_____

_____

_____

_____

_____

_____

_____

_____

_____

_____

Day: _____ Date: _____

Sprinkle of the Day: _____

Sprinkle Affirmation: _____

_____

_____

1. Today I am grateful for: _____

_____

_____

2. My intention for today is: _____

_____

_____

3. A challenge I might face today and how I will approach it:

_____

_____

4. One thought or belief I'm letting go of today is:

_____

_____

5. One thing I will do today to bring joy into my life is:

_____

_____

Sprinkle Reflection:

_____

_____

_____

_____

_____

_____

_____

_____

_____

_____

_____

_____

_____

_____

_____

_____

_____

_____

_____

_____

_____

Day: _____ Date: _____

Sprinkle of the Day: _____

Sprinkle Affirmation: _____

_____

_____

1. Today I am grateful for: _____

_____

_____

2. My intention for today is: _____

_____

_____

3. A challenge I might face today and how I will approach it:

_____

_____

4. One thought or belief I'm letting go of today is:

_____

_____

5. One thing I will do today to bring joy into my life is:

_____

_____

Sprinkle Reflection:

_____

_____

_____

_____

_____

_____

_____

_____

_____

_____

_____

_____

_____

_____

_____

_____

_____

_____

_____

_____

_____

_____

Day: _____ Date: _____

Sprinkle of the Day: _____

Sprinkle Affirmation: _____

_____

_____

1. Today I am grateful for: _____

_____

_____

2. My intention for today is: _____

_____

_____

3. A challenge I might face today and how I will approach it:

_____

_____

4. One thought or belief I'm letting go of today is:

_____

_____

5. One thing I will do today to bring joy into my life is:

_____

_____

Sprinkle Reflection:

_____

_____

_____

_____

_____

_____

_____

_____

_____

_____

_____

_____

_____

_____

_____

_____

_____

_____

_____

_____

Day: _____ Date: _____

Sprinkle of the Day: _____

Sprinkle Affirmation: _____

_____

_____

1. Today I am grateful for: _____

_____

_____

2. My intention for today is: _____

_____

_____

3. A challenge I might face today and how I will approach it:

_____

_____

4. One thought or belief I'm letting go of today is:

_____

_____

5. One thing I will do today to bring joy into my life is:

_____

_____

Sprinkle Reflection:

_____

_____

_____

_____

_____

_____

_____

_____

_____

_____

_____

_____

_____

_____

_____

_____

_____

_____

_____

_____

_____

_____

Day: _____ Date: _____

Sprinkle of the Day: _____

Sprinkle Affirmation: _____

_____

_____

1. Today I am grateful for: _____

_____

_____

2. My intention for today is: _____

_____

_____

3. A challenge I might face today and how I will approach it:

_____

_____

4. One thought or belief I'm letting go of today is:

_____

_____

5. One thing I will do today to bring joy into my life is:

_____

_____

Sprinkle Reflection:

_____

_____

_____

_____

_____

_____

_____

_____

_____

_____

_____

_____

_____

_____

_____

_____

_____

_____

_____

_____

_____

Day: _____ Date: _____

Sprinkle of the Day: _____

Sprinkle Affirmation: _____

_____

_____

1. Today I am grateful for: _____

_____

_____

2. My intention for today is: _____

_____

_____

3. A challenge I might face today and how I will approach it:

_____

_____

4. One thought or belief I'm letting go of today is:

_____

_____

5. One thing I will do today to bring joy into my life is:

_____

_____

Sprinkle Reflection:

_____

_____

_____

_____

_____

_____

_____

_____

_____

_____

_____

_____

_____

_____

_____

_____

_____

_____

_____

_____

_____

_____

Day: _____ Date: _____

Sprinkle of the Day: _____

Sprinkle Affirmation: _____

_____

_____

1. Today I am grateful for: _____

_____

_____

2. My intention for today is: _____

_____

_____

3. A challenge I might face today and how I will approach it:

_____

_____

4. One thought or belief I'm letting go of today is:

_____

_____

5. One thing I will do today to bring joy into my life is:

_____

_____

Sprinkle Reflection:

_____

_____

_____

_____

_____

_____

_____

_____

_____

_____

_____

_____

_____

_____

_____

_____

_____

_____

_____

_____

_____

Day: _____ Date: _____

Sprinkle of the Day: _____

Sprinkle Affirmation: _____

_____

_____

1. Today I am grateful for: _____

_____

_____

2. My intention for today is: _____

_____

_____

3. A challenge I might face today and how I will approach it:

_____

_____

4. One thought or belief I'm letting go of today is:

_____

_____

5. One thing I will do today to bring joy into my life is:

_____

_____

Sprinkle Reflection:

_____

_____

_____

_____

_____

_____

_____

_____

_____

_____

_____

_____

_____

_____

_____

_____

_____

_____

_____

_____

_____

Day: _____ Date: _____

Sprinkle of the Day: _____

Sprinkle Affirmation: _____

_____

_____

1. Today I am grateful for: _____

_____

_____

2. My intention for today is: _____

_____

_____

3. A challenge I might face today and how I will approach it:

_____

_____

4. One thought or belief I'm letting go of today is:

_____

_____

5. One thing I will do today to bring joy into my life is:

_____

_____

Sprinkle Reflection:

_____

_____

_____

_____

_____

_____

_____

_____

_____

_____

_____

_____

_____

_____

_____

_____

_____

_____

_____

Day: _____ Date: _____

Sprinkle of the Day: _____

Sprinkle Affirmation: _____

_____

_____

1. Today I am grateful for: _____

_____

_____

2. My intention for today is: _____

_____

_____

3. A challenge I might face today and how I will approach it:

_____

_____

4. One thought or belief I'm letting go of today is:

_____

_____

5. One thing I will do today to bring joy into my life is:

_____

_____

Sprinkle Reflection:

_____

_____

_____

_____

_____

_____

_____

_____

_____

_____

_____

_____

_____

_____

_____

_____

_____

_____

_____

_____

_____

_____

Day: _____ Date: _____

Sprinkle of the Day: _____

Sprinkle Affirmation: _____

_____

_____

1. Today I am grateful for: _____

_____

_____

2. My intention for today is: _____

_____

_____

3. A challenge I might face today and how I will approach it:

_____

_____

4. One thought or belief I'm letting go of today is:

_____

_____

5. One thing I will do today to bring joy into my life is:

_____

_____

Sprinkle Reflection:

_____

_____

_____

_____

_____

_____

_____

_____

_____

_____

_____

_____

_____

_____

_____

_____

_____

_____

_____

_____

Day: _____ Date: _____

Sprinkle of the Day: _____

Sprinkle Affirmation: _____

_____

_____

1. Today I am grateful for: _____

_____

_____

2. My intention for today is: _____

_____

_____

3. A challenge I might face today and how I will approach it:

_____

_____

4. One thought or belief I'm letting go of today is:

_____

_____

5. One thing I will do today to bring joy into my life is:

_____

_____

Sprinkle Reflection:

_____

_____

_____

_____

_____

_____

_____

_____

_____

_____

_____

_____

_____

_____

_____

_____

_____

_____

_____

_____

Day: _____ Date: _____

Sprinkle of the Day: _____

Sprinkle Affirmation: _____

_____

_____

1. Today I am grateful for: _____

_____

_____

2. My intention for today is: _____

_____

_____

3. A challenge I might face today and how I will approach it:

_____

_____

4. One thought or belief I'm letting go of today is:

_____

_____

5. One thing I will do today to bring joy into my life is:

_____

_____

Sprinkle Reflection:

_____

_____

_____

_____

_____

_____

_____

_____

_____

_____

_____

_____

_____

_____

_____

_____

_____

_____

_____

_____

_____

_____

Day: _____ Date: _____

Sprinkle of the Day: _____

Sprinkle Affirmation: _____

_____

_____

1. Today I am grateful for: _____

_____

_____

2. My intention for today is: _____

_____

_____

3. A challenge I might face today and how I will approach it:

_____

_____

4. One thought or belief I'm letting go of today is:

_____

_____

5. One thing I will do today to bring joy into my life is:

_____

_____

Sprinkle Reflection:

_____
_____
_____
_____
_____
_____
_____
_____
_____
_____
_____
_____
_____
_____
_____
_____
_____
_____
_____
_____
_____

Day: _____ Date: _____

Sprinkle of the Day: _____

Sprinkle Affirmation: _____

_____

_____

1. Today I am grateful for: _____

_____

_____

2. My intention for today is: _____

_____

_____

3. A challenge I might face today and how I will approach it:

_____

_____

4. One thought or belief I'm letting go of today is:

_____

_____

5. One thing I will do today to bring joy into my life is:

_____

_____

Sprinkle Reflection:

_____

_____

_____

_____

_____

_____

_____

_____

_____

_____

_____

_____

_____

_____

_____

_____

_____

_____

_____

_____

Day: _____ Date: _____

Sprinkle of the Day: _____

Sprinkle Affirmation: _____

_____

_____

1. Today I am grateful for: _____

_____

_____

2. My intention for today is: _____

_____

_____

3. A challenge I might face today and how I will approach it:

_____

_____

4. One thought or belief I'm letting go of today is:

_____

_____

5. One thing I will do today to bring joy into my life is:

_____

_____

Sprinkle Reflection:

_____

_____

_____

_____

_____

_____

_____

_____

_____

_____

_____

_____

_____

_____

_____

_____

_____

_____

_____

_____

_____

Day: _____ Date: _____

Sprinkle of the Day: _____

Sprinkle Affirmation: _____

_____

_____

1. Today I am grateful for: _____

_____

_____

2. My intention for today is: _____

_____

_____

3. A challenge I might face today and how I will approach it:

_____

_____

4. One thought or belief I'm letting go of today is:

_____

_____

5. One thing I will do today to bring joy into my life is:

_____

_____

Sprinkle Reflection:

_____

_____

_____

_____

_____

_____

_____

_____

_____

_____

_____

_____

_____

_____

_____

_____

_____

_____

Day: _____ Date: _____

Sprinkle of the Day: _____

Sprinkle Affirmation: _____

_____

_____

1. Today I am grateful for: _____

_____

_____

2. My intention for today is: _____

_____

_____

3. A challenge I might face today and how I will approach it:

_____

_____

4. One thought or belief I'm letting go of today is:

_____

_____

5. One thing I will do today to bring joy into my life is:

_____

_____

Sprinkle Reflection:

_____

_____

_____

_____

_____

_____

_____

_____

_____

_____

_____

_____

_____

_____

_____

_____

_____

_____

_____

_____

Day: _____ Date: _____

Sprinkle of the Day: _____

Sprinkle Affirmation: _____

_____

_____

1. Today I am grateful for: _____

_____

_____

2. My intention for today is: _____

_____

_____

3. A challenge I might face today and how I will approach it:

_____

_____

4. One thought or belief I'm letting go of today is:

_____

_____

5. One thing I will do today to bring joy into my life is:

_____

_____

Sprinkle Reflection:

_____

_____

_____

_____

_____

_____

_____

_____

_____

_____

_____

_____

_____

_____

_____

_____

_____

_____

_____

_____

Day: _____ Date: _____

Sprinkle of the Day: _____

Sprinkle Affirmation: _____

_____

_____

1. Today I am grateful for: _____

_____

_____

2. My intention for today is: _____

_____

_____

3. A challenge I might face today and how I will approach it:

_____

_____

4. One thought or belief I'm letting go of today is:

_____

_____

5. One thing I will do today to bring joy into my life is:

_____

_____

Sprinkle Reflection:

_____

_____

_____

_____

_____

_____

_____

_____

_____

_____

_____

_____

_____

_____

_____

_____

_____

_____

Day: _____ Date: _____

Sprinkle of the Day: _____

Sprinkle Affirmation: _____

_____

_____

1. Today I am grateful for: _____

_____

_____

2. My intention for today is: _____

_____

_____

3. A challenge I might face today and how I will approach it:

_____

_____

4. One thought or belief I'm letting go of today is:

_____

_____

5. One thing I will do today to bring joy into my life is:

_____

_____

Sprinkle Reflection:

_____

_____

_____

_____

_____

_____

_____

_____

_____

_____

_____

_____

_____

_____

_____

_____

_____

_____

_____

_____

_____

_____

Day: _____ Date: _____

Sprinkle of the Day: _____

Sprinkle Affirmation: _____

_____

_____

1. Today I am grateful for: _____

_____

_____

2. My intention for today is: _____

_____

_____

3. A challenge I might face today and how I will approach it:

_____

_____

4. One thought or belief I'm letting go of today is:

_____

_____

5. One thing I will do today to bring joy into my life is:

_____

_____

Sprinkle Reflection:

_____

_____

_____

_____

_____

_____

_____

_____

_____

_____

_____

_____

_____

_____

_____

_____

_____

_____

_____

_____

Day: _____ Date: _____

Sprinkle of the Day: _____

Sprinkle Affirmation: _____

_____

_____

1. Today I am grateful for: _____

_____

_____

2. My intention for today is: _____

_____

_____

3. A challenge I might face today and how I will approach it:

_____

_____

4. One thought or belief I'm letting go of today is:

_____

_____

5. One thing I will do today to bring joy into my life is:

_____

_____

Sprinkle Reflection:

_____

_____

_____

_____

_____

_____

_____

_____

_____

_____

_____

_____

_____

_____

_____

_____

_____

_____

_____

Day: _____ Date: _____

Sprinkle of the Day: _____

Sprinkle Affirmation: _____

_____

_____

1. Today I am grateful for: _____

_____

_____

2. My intention for today is: _____

_____

_____

3. A challenge I might face today and how I will approach it:

_____

_____

4. One thought or belief I'm letting go of today is:

_____

_____

5. One thing I will do today to bring joy into my life is:

_____

_____

Sprinkle Reflection:

_____

_____

_____

_____

_____

_____

_____

_____

_____

_____

_____

_____

_____

_____

_____

_____

_____

_____

_____

Day: _____ Date: _____

Sprinkle of the Day: _____

Sprinkle Affirmation: _____

_____

_____

1. Today I am grateful for: _____

_____

_____

2. My intention for today is: _____

_____

_____

3. A challenge I might face today and how I will approach it:

_____

_____

4. One thought or belief I'm letting go of today is:

_____

_____

5. One thing I will do today to bring joy into my life is:

_____

_____

Sprinkle Reflection:

_____

_____

_____

_____

_____

_____

_____

_____

_____

_____

_____

_____

_____

_____

_____

_____

_____

_____

_____

_____

_____

_____

Day: _____ Date: _____

Sprinkle of the Day: _____

Sprinkle Affirmation: _____

_____

_____

1. Today I am grateful for: _____

_____

_____

2. My intention for today is: _____

_____

_____

3. A challenge I might face today and how I will approach it:

_____

_____

4. One thought or belief I'm letting go of today is:

_____

_____

5. One thing I will do today to bring joy into my life is:

_____

_____

Sprinkle Reflection:

_____

_____

_____

_____

_____

_____

_____

_____

_____

_____

_____

_____

_____

_____

_____

_____

_____

_____

Day: _____ Date: _____

Sprinkle of the Day: _____

Sprinkle Affirmation: _____

_____

_____

1. Today I am grateful for: _____

_____

_____

2. My intention for today is: _____

_____

_____

3. A challenge I might face today and how I will approach it:

_____

_____

4. One thought or belief I'm letting go of today is:

_____

_____

5. One thing I will do today to bring joy into my life is:

_____

_____

Sprinkle Reflection:

_____
_____
_____
_____
_____
_____
_____
_____
_____
_____
_____
_____
_____
_____
_____
_____
_____
_____

Day: _____ Date: _____

Sprinkle of the Day: _____

Sprinkle Affirmation: _____

_____

_____

1. Today I am grateful for: _____

_____

_____

2. My intention for today is: _____

_____

_____

3. A challenge I might face today and how I will approach it:

_____

_____

4. One thought or belief I'm letting go of today is:

_____

_____

5. One thing I will do today to bring joy into my life is:

_____

_____

Sprinkle Reflection:

_____

_____

_____

_____

_____

_____

_____

_____

_____

_____

_____

_____

_____

_____

_____

_____

_____

_____

_____

_____

Day: _____ Date: _____

Sprinkle of the Day: _____

Sprinkle Affirmation: _____

_____

_____

1. Today I am grateful for: _____

_____

_____

2. My intention for today is: _____

_____

_____

3. A challenge I might face today and how I will approach it:

_____

_____

4. One thought or belief I'm letting go of today is:

_____

_____

5. One thing I will do today to bring joy into my life is:

_____

_____

Sprinkle Reflection:

_____

_____

_____

_____

_____

_____

_____

_____

_____

_____

_____

_____

_____

_____

_____

_____

_____

_____

_____

_____

Day: _____ Date: _____

Sprinkle of the Day: _____

Sprinkle Affirmation: _____

_____

_____

1. Today I am grateful for: _____

_____

_____

2. My intention for today is: _____

_____

_____

3. A challenge I might face today and how I will approach it:

_____

_____

4. One thought or belief I'm letting go of today is:

_____

_____

5. One thing I will do today to bring joy into my life is:

_____

_____

Sprinkle Reflection:

_____

_____

_____

_____

_____

_____

_____

_____

_____

_____

_____

_____

_____

_____

_____

_____

_____

_____

_____

_____

_____

Day: _____ Date: _____

Sprinkle of the Day: _____

Sprinkle Affirmation: _____

_____

_____

1. Today I am grateful for: _____

_____

_____

2. My intention for today is: _____

_____

_____

3. A challenge I might face today and how I will approach it:

_____

_____

4. One thought or belief I'm letting go of today is:

_____

_____

5. One thing I will do today to bring joy into my life is:

_____

_____

Sprinkle Reflection:

_____

_____

_____

_____

_____

_____

_____

_____

_____

_____

_____

_____

_____

_____

_____

_____

_____

_____

_____

_____

Day: _____ Date: _____

Sprinkle of the Day: _____

Sprinkle Affirmation: _____

_____

_____

1. Today I am grateful for: _____

_____

_____

2. My intention for today is: _____

_____

_____

3. A challenge I might face today and how I will approach it:

_____

_____

4. One thought or belief I'm letting go of today is:

_____

_____

5. One thing I will do today to bring joy into my life is:

_____

_____

Sprinkle Reflection:

_____

_____

_____

_____

_____

_____

_____

_____

_____

_____

_____

_____

_____

_____

_____

_____

_____

_____

_____

_____

_____

Day: _____ Date: _____

Sprinkle of the Day: _____

Sprinkle Affirmation: _____

_____

_____

1. Today I am grateful for: _____

_____

_____

2. My intention for today is: _____

_____

_____

3. A challenge I might face today and how I will approach it:

_____

_____

4. One thought or belief I'm letting go of today is:

_____

_____

5. One thing I will do today to bring joy into my life is:

_____

_____

Sprinkle Reflection:

_____

_____

_____

_____

_____

_____

_____

_____

_____

_____

_____

_____

_____

_____

_____

_____

_____

_____

_____

_____

Day: _____ Date: _____

Sprinkle of the Day: _____

Sprinkle Affirmation: _____

_____

_____

1. Today I am grateful for: _____

_____

_____

2. My intention for today is: _____

_____

_____

3. A challenge I might face today and how I will approach it:

_____

_____

4. One thought or belief I'm letting go of today is:

_____

_____

5. One thing I will do today to bring joy into my life is:

_____

_____

Sprinkle Reflection:

_____

_____

_____

_____

_____

_____

_____

_____

_____

_____

_____

_____

_____

_____

_____

_____

_____

_____

_____

_____

_____

Day: _____ Date: _____

Sprinkle of the Day: _____

Sprinkle Affirmation: _____

_____

_____

1. Today I am grateful for: _____

_____

_____

2. My intention for today is: _____

_____

_____

3. A challenge I might face today and how I will approach it:

_____

_____

4. One thought or belief I'm letting go of today is:

_____

_____

5. One thing I will do today to bring joy into my life is:

_____

_____

Sprinkle Reflection:

_____

_____

_____

_____

_____

_____

_____

_____

_____

_____

_____

_____

_____

_____

_____

_____

_____

_____

_____

Day: _____ Date: _____

Sprinkle of the Day: _____

Sprinkle Affirmation: _____

_____

_____

1. Today I am grateful for: _____

_____

_____

2. My intention for today is: _____

_____

_____

3. A challenge I might face today and how I will approach it:

_____

_____

4. One thought or belief I'm letting go of today is:

_____

_____

5. One thing I will do today to bring joy into my life is:

_____

_____

Sprinkle Reflection:

_____

_____

_____

_____

_____

_____

_____

_____

_____

_____

_____

_____

_____

_____

_____

_____

_____

_____

_____

Day: _____ Date: _____

Sprinkle of the Day: _____

Sprinkle Affirmation: _____

_____

_____

1. Today I am grateful for: _____

_____

_____

2. My intention for today is: _____

_____

_____

3. A challenge I might face today and how I will approach it:

_____

_____

4. One thought or belief I'm letting go of today is:

_____

_____

5. One thing I will do today to bring joy into my life is:

_____

_____

Sprinkle Reflection:

_____

_____

_____

_____

_____

_____

_____

_____

_____

_____

_____

_____

_____

_____

_____

_____

_____

_____

_____

Day: _____ Date: _____

Sprinkle of the Day: _____

Sprinkle Affirmation: _____

_____

_____

1. Today I am grateful for: _____

_____

_____

2. My intention for today is: _____

_____

_____

3. A challenge I might face today and how I will approach it:

_____

_____

4. One thought or belief I'm letting go of today is:

_____

_____

5. One thing I will do today to bring joy into my life is:

_____

_____

Sprinkle Reflection:

_____

_____

_____

_____

_____

_____

_____

_____

_____

_____

_____

_____

_____

_____

_____

_____

_____

_____

_____

_____

_____

Day: _____ Date: _____

Sprinkle of the Day: _____

Sprinkle Affirmation: _____

_____

_____

1. Today I am grateful for: _____

_____

_____

2. My intention for today is: _____

_____

_____

3. A challenge I might face today and how I will approach it:

_____

_____

4. One thought or belief I'm letting go of today is:

_____

_____

5. One thing I will do today to bring joy into my life is:

_____

_____

Sprinkle Reflection:

_____

_____

_____

_____

_____

_____

_____

_____

_____

_____

_____

_____

_____

_____

_____

_____

_____

_____

_____

_____

Day: _____ Date: _____

Sprinkle of the Day: _____

Sprinkle Affirmation: _____

_____

_____

1. Today I am grateful for: _____

_____

_____

2. My intention for today is: _____

_____

_____

3. A challenge I might face today and how I will approach it:

_____

_____

4. One thought or belief I'm letting go of today is:

_____

_____

5. One thing I will do today to bring joy into my life is:

_____

_____

Sprinkle Reflection:

_____

_____

_____

_____

_____

_____

_____

_____

_____

_____

_____

_____

_____

_____

_____

_____

_____

_____

_____

_____

_____

_____

Day: _____ Date: _____

Sprinkle of the Day: _____

Sprinkle Affirmation: _____

_____

_____

1. Today I am grateful for: _____

_____

_____

2. My intention for today is: _____

_____

_____

3. A challenge I might face today and how I will approach it:

_____

_____

4. One thought or belief I'm letting go of today is:

_____

_____

5. One thing I will do today to bring joy into my life is:

_____

_____

Sprinkle Reflection:

_____

_____

_____

_____

_____

_____

_____

_____

_____

_____

_____

_____

_____

_____

_____

_____

_____

_____

_____

_____

Day: _____ Date: _____

Sprinkle of the Day: _____

Sprinkle Affirmation: _____

_____

_____

1. Today I am grateful for: _____

_____

_____

2. My intention for today is: _____

_____

_____

3. A challenge I might face today and how I will approach it:

_____

_____

4. One thought or belief I'm letting go of today is:

_____

_____

5. One thing I will do today to bring joy into my life is:

_____

_____

Sprinkle Reflection:

_____

_____

_____

_____

_____

_____

_____

_____

_____

_____

_____

_____

_____

_____

_____

_____

_____

_____

_____

_____

Day: _____ Date: _____

Sprinkle of the Day: _____

Sprinkle Affirmation: _____

_____

_____

1. Today I am grateful for: _____

_____

_____

2. My intention for today is: _____

_____

_____

3. A challenge I might face today and how I will approach it:

_____

_____

4. One thought or belief I'm letting go of today is:

_____

_____

5. One thing I will do today to bring joy into my life is:

_____

_____

Sprinkle Reflection:

_____

_____

_____

_____

_____

_____

_____

_____

_____

_____

_____

_____

_____

_____

_____

_____

_____

_____

_____

_____

_____

_____

Day: _____ Date: _____

Sprinkle of the Day: _____

Sprinkle Affirmation: _____

_____

_____

1. Today I am grateful for: _____

_____

_____

2. My intention for today is: _____

_____

_____

3. A challenge I might face today and how I will approach it:

_____

_____

4. One thought or belief I'm letting go of today is:

_____

_____

5. One thing I will do today to bring joy into my life is:

_____

_____

Sprinkle Reflection:

_____

_____

_____

_____

_____

_____

_____

_____

_____

_____

_____

_____

_____

_____

_____

_____

_____

_____

_____

Day: _____ Date: _____

Sprinkle of the Day: _____

Sprinkle Affirmation: _____

_____

_____

1. Today I am grateful for: _____

_____

_____

2. My intention for today is: _____

_____

_____

3. A challenge I might face today and how I will approach it:

_____

_____

4. One thought or belief I'm letting go of today is:

_____

_____

5. One thing I will do today to bring joy into my life is:

_____

_____

Sprinkle Reflection:

_____

_____

_____

_____

_____

_____

_____

_____

_____

_____

_____

_____

_____

_____

_____

_____

_____

_____

_____

Day: _____ Date: _____

Sprinkle of the Day: _____

Sprinkle Affirmation: _____

_____

_____

1. Today I am grateful for: _____

_____

_____

2. My intention for today is: _____

_____

_____

3. A challenge I might face today and how I will approach it:

_____

_____

4. One thought or belief I'm letting go of today is:

_____

_____

5. One thing I will do today to bring joy into my life is:

_____

_____

Sprinkle Reflection:

_____
_____
_____
_____
_____
_____
_____
_____
_____
_____
_____
_____
_____
_____
_____
_____
_____
_____
_____
_____
_____
_____

Day: _____ Date: _____

Sprinkle of the Day: _____

Sprinkle Affirmation: _____

_____

_____

1. Today I am grateful for: _____

_____

_____

2. My intention for today is: _____

_____

_____

3. A challenge I might face today and how I will approach it:

_____

_____

4. One thought or belief I'm letting go of today is:

_____

_____

5. One thing I will do today to bring joy into my life is:

_____

_____

Sprinkle Reflection:

_____

_____

_____

_____

_____

_____

_____

_____

_____

_____

_____

_____

_____

_____

_____

_____

_____

_____

_____

_____

Day: _____ Date: _____

Sprinkle of the Day: _____

Sprinkle Affirmation: _____

_____

_____

1. Today I am grateful for: _____

_____

_____

2. My intention for today is: _____

_____

_____

3. A challenge I might face today and how I will approach it:

_____

_____

4. One thought or belief I'm letting go of today is:

_____

_____

5. One thing I will do today to bring joy into my life is:

_____

_____

Sprinkle Reflection:

_____

_____

_____

_____

_____

_____

_____

_____

_____

_____

_____

_____

_____

_____

_____

_____

_____

_____

_____

Day: _____ Date: _____

Sprinkle of the Day: _____

Sprinkle Affirmation: _____

_____

_____

1. Today I am grateful for: _____

_____

_____

2. My intention for today is: _____

_____

_____

3. A challenge I might face today and how I will approach it:

_____

_____

4. One thought or belief I'm letting go of today is:

_____

_____

5. One thing I will do today to bring joy into my life is:

_____

_____

Sprinkle Reflection:

_____
_____
_____
_____
_____
_____
_____
_____
_____
_____
_____
_____
_____
_____
_____
_____
_____
_____
_____
_____
_____
_____

Day: _____ Date: _____

Sprinkle of the Day: _____

Sprinkle Affirmation: _____

_____

_____

1. Today I am grateful for: _____

_____

_____

2. My intention for today is: _____

_____

_____

3. A challenge I might face today and how I will approach it:

_____

_____

4. One thought or belief I'm letting go of today is:

_____

_____

5. One thing I will do today to bring joy into my life is:

_____

_____

Sprinkle Reflection:

_____

_____

_____

_____

_____

_____

_____

_____

_____

_____

_____

_____

_____

_____

_____

_____

_____

_____

Day: _____ Date: _____

Sprinkle of the Day: _____

Sprinkle Affirmation: _____

_____

_____

1. Today I am grateful for: _____

_____

_____

2. My intention for today is: _____

_____

_____

3. A challenge I might face today and how I will approach it:

_____

_____

4. One thought or belief I'm letting go of today is:

_____

_____

5. One thing I will do today to bring joy into my life is:

_____

_____

Sprinkle Reflection:

_____
_____
_____
_____
_____
_____
_____
_____
_____
_____
_____
_____
_____
_____
_____
_____
_____
_____
_____
_____

Day: _____ Date: _____

Sprinkle of the Day: _____

Sprinkle Affirmation: _____

_____

_____

1. Today I am grateful for: _____

_____

_____

2. My intention for today is: _____

_____

_____

3. A challenge I might face today and how I will approach it:

_____

_____

4. One thought or belief I'm letting go of today is:

_____

_____

5. One thing I will do today to bring joy into my life is:

_____

_____

Sprinkle Reflection:

_____

_____

_____

_____

_____

_____

_____

_____

_____

_____

_____

_____

_____

_____

_____

_____

_____

_____

_____

_____

_____

Day: _____ Date: _____

Sprinkle of the Day: _____

Sprinkle Affirmation: _____

_____

_____

1. Today I am grateful for: _____

_____

_____

2. My intention for today is: _____

_____

_____

3. A challenge I might face today and how I will approach it:

_____

_____

4. One thought or belief I'm letting go of today is:

_____

_____

5. One thing I will do today to bring joy into my life is:

_____

_____

Sprinkle Reflection:

_____

_____

_____

_____

_____

_____

_____

_____

_____

_____

_____

_____

_____

_____

_____

_____

_____

_____

_____

Day: _____ Date: _____

Sprinkle of the Day: _____

Sprinkle Affirmation: _____

_____

_____

1. Today I am grateful for: _____

_____

_____

2. My intention for today is: _____

_____

_____

3. A challenge I might face today and how I will approach it:

_____

_____

4. One thought or belief I'm letting go of today is:

_____

_____

5. One thing I will do today to bring joy into my life is:

_____

_____

Sprinkle Reflection:

_____

_____

_____

_____

_____

_____

_____

_____

_____

_____

_____

_____

_____

_____

_____

_____

_____

_____

_____

_____

_____

Day: _____ Date: _____

Sprinkle of the Day: _____

Sprinkle Affirmation: _____

_____

_____

1. Today I am grateful for: _____

_____

_____

2. My intention for today is: _____

_____

_____

3. A challenge I might face today and how I will approach it:

_____

_____

4. One thought or belief I'm letting go of today is:

_____

_____

5. One thing I will do today to bring joy into my life is:

_____

_____

Sprinkle Reflection:

_____

_____

_____

_____

_____

_____

_____

_____

_____

_____

_____

_____

_____

_____

_____

_____

_____

_____

_____

_____

_____

_____

Day: _____ Date: _____

Sprinkle of the Day: _____

Sprinkle Affirmation: _____

_____

_____

1. Today I am grateful for: _____

_____

_____

2. My intention for today is: _____

_____

_____

3. A challenge I might face today and how I will approach it:

_____

_____

4. One thought or belief I'm letting go of today is:

_____

_____

5. One thing I will do today to bring joy into my life is:

_____

_____

Sprinkle Reflection:

_____

_____

_____

_____

_____

_____

_____

_____

_____

_____

_____

_____

_____

_____

_____

_____

_____

_____

_____

Day: _____ Date: _____

Sprinkle of the Day: _____

Sprinkle Affirmation: _____

_____

_____

1. Today I am grateful for: _____

_____

_____

2. My intention for today is: _____

_____

_____

3. A challenge I might face today and how I will approach it:

_____

_____

4. One thought or belief I'm letting go of today is:

_____

_____

5. One thing I will do today to bring joy into my life is:

_____

_____

Sprinkle Reflection:

_____

_____

_____

_____

_____

_____

_____

_____

_____

_____

_____

_____

_____

_____

_____

_____

_____

_____

_____

_____

Day: _____ Date: _____

Sprinkle of the Day: _____

Sprinkle Affirmation: _____

_____

_____

1. Today I am grateful for: _____

_____

_____

2. My intention for today is: _____

_____

_____

3. A challenge I might face today and how I will approach it:

_____

_____

4. One thought or belief I'm letting go of today is:

_____

_____

5. One thing I will do today to bring joy into my life is:

_____

_____

Sprinkle Reflection:

_____

_____

_____

_____

_____

_____

_____

_____

_____

_____

_____

_____

_____

_____

_____

_____

_____

_____

_____

_____

_____

Day: _____ Date: _____

Sprinkle of the Day: _____

Sprinkle Affirmation: _____

_____

_____

1. Today I am grateful for: _____

_____

_____

2. My intention for today is: _____

_____

_____

3. A challenge I might face today and how I will approach it:

_____

_____

4. One thought or belief I'm letting go of today is:

_____

_____

5. One thing I will do today to bring joy into my life is:

_____

_____

Sprinkle Reflection:

_____

_____

_____

_____

_____

_____

_____

_____

_____

_____

_____

_____

_____

_____

_____

_____

_____

_____

_____

Day: _____ Date: _____

Sprinkle of the Day: _____

Sprinkle Affirmation: _____

_____

_____

1. Today I am grateful for: _____

_____

_____

2. My intention for today is: _____

_____

_____

3. A challenge I might face today and how I will approach it:

_____

_____

4. One thought or belief I'm letting go of today is:

_____

_____

5. One thing I will do today to bring joy into my life is:

_____

_____

Sprinkle Reflection:

_____

_____

_____

_____

_____

_____

_____

_____

_____

_____

_____

_____

_____

_____

_____

_____

_____

_____

_____

_____

_____

Day: _____ Date: _____

Sprinkle of the Day: _____

Sprinkle Affirmation: _____

_____

_____

1. Today I am grateful for: _____

_____

_____

2. My intention for today is: _____

_____

_____

3. A challenge I might face today and how I will approach it:

_____

_____

4. One thought or belief I'm letting go of today is:

_____

_____

5. One thing I will do today to bring joy into my life is:

_____

_____

Sprinkle Reflection:

_____

_____

_____

_____

_____

_____

_____

_____

_____

_____

_____

_____

_____

_____

_____

_____

_____

_____

_____

_____

Day: _____ Date: _____

Sprinkle of the Day: _____

Sprinkle Affirmation: _____

_____

_____

1. Today I am grateful for: _____

_____

_____

2. My intention for today is: _____

_____

_____

3. A challenge I might face today and how I will approach it:

_____

_____

4. One thought or belief I'm letting go of today is:

_____

_____

5. One thing I will do today to bring joy into my life is:

_____

_____

Sprinkle Reflection:

_____

_____

_____

_____

_____

_____

_____

_____

_____

_____

_____

_____

_____

_____

_____

_____

_____

_____

_____

_____

Day: _____ Date: _____

Sprinkle of the Day: _____

Sprinkle Affirmation: _____

_____

_____

1. Today I am grateful for: _____

_____

_____

2. My intention for today is: _____

_____

_____

3. A challenge I might face today and how I will approach it:

_____

_____

4. One thought or belief I'm letting go of today is:

_____

_____

5. One thing I will do today to bring joy into my life is:

_____

_____

Sprinkle Reflection:

_____

_____

_____

_____

_____

_____

_____

_____

_____

_____

_____

_____

_____

_____

_____

_____

_____

_____

_____

Day: _____ Date: _____

Sprinkle of the Day: _____

Sprinkle Affirmation: _____

_____

_____

1. Today I am grateful for: _____

_____

_____

2. My intention for today is: _____

_____

_____

3. A challenge I might face today and how I will approach it:

_____

_____

4. One thought or belief I'm letting go of today is:

_____

_____

5. One thing I will do today to bring joy into my life is:

_____

_____

Sprinkle Reflection:

_____

_____

_____

_____

_____

_____

_____

_____

_____

_____

_____

_____

_____

_____

_____

_____

_____

_____

_____

_____

_____

_____

Day: _____ Date: _____

Sprinkle of the Day: _____

Sprinkle Affirmation: _____

_____

_____

1. Today I am grateful for: _____

_____

_____

2. My intention for today is: _____

_____

_____

3. A challenge I might face today and how I will approach it:

_____

_____

4. One thought or belief I'm letting go of today is:

_____

_____

5. One thing I will do today to bring joy into my life is:

_____

_____

Sprinkle Reflection:

_____

_____

_____

_____

_____

_____

_____

_____

_____

_____

_____

_____

_____

_____

_____

_____

_____

_____

_____

Day: _____ Date: _____

Sprinkle of the Day: _____

Sprinkle Affirmation: _____

_____

_____

1. Today I am grateful for: _____

_____

_____

2. My intention for today is: _____

_____

_____

3. A challenge I might face today and how I will approach it:

_____

_____

4. One thought or belief I'm letting go of today is:

_____

_____

5. One thing I will do today to bring joy into my life is:

_____

_____

Sprinkle Reflection:

_____

_____

_____

_____

_____

_____

_____

_____

_____

_____

_____

_____

_____

_____

_____

_____

_____

_____

_____

Day: _____ Date: _____

Sprinkle of the Day: _____

Sprinkle Affirmation: _____

_____

_____

1. Today I am grateful for: _____

_____

_____

2. My intention for today is: _____

_____

_____

3. A challenge I might face today and how I will approach it:

_____

_____

4. One thought or belief I'm letting go of today is:

_____

_____

5. One thing I will do today to bring joy into my life is:

_____

_____

Sprinkle Reflection:

_____

_____

_____

_____

_____

_____

_____

_____

_____

_____

_____

_____

_____

_____

_____

_____

_____

_____

_____

_____

_____

Day: _____ Date: _____

Sprinkle of the Day: _____

Sprinkle Affirmation: _____

_____

_____

1. Today I am grateful for: _____

_____

_____

2. My intention for today is: _____

_____

_____

3. A challenge I might face today and how I will approach it:

_____

_____

4. One thought or belief I'm letting go of today is:

_____

_____

5. One thing I will do today to bring joy into my life is:

_____

_____

Sprinkle Reflection:

_____

_____

_____

_____

_____

_____

_____

_____

_____

_____

_____

_____

_____

_____

_____

_____

_____

_____

_____

Day: _____ Date: _____

Sprinkle of the Day: _____

Sprinkle Affirmation: _____

_____

_____

1. Today I am grateful for: _____

_____

_____

2. My intention for today is: _____

_____

_____

3. A challenge I might face today and how I will approach it:

_____

_____

4. One thought or belief I'm letting go of today is:

_____

_____

5. One thing I will do today to bring joy into my life is:

_____

_____

Sprinkle Reflection:

_____

_____

_____

_____

_____

_____

_____

_____

_____

_____

_____

_____

_____

_____

_____

_____

_____

_____

_____

Day: _____ Date: _____

Sprinkle of the Day: _____

Sprinkle Affirmation: _____

_____

_____

1. Today I am grateful for: _____

_____

_____

2. My intention for today is: _____

_____

_____

3. A challenge I might face today and how I will approach it:

_____

_____

4. One thought or belief I'm letting go of today is:

_____

_____

5. One thing I will do today to bring joy into my life is:

_____

_____

Sprinkle Reflection:

_____

_____

_____

_____

_____

_____

_____

_____

_____

_____

_____

_____

_____

_____

_____

_____

_____

_____

_____

_____

Day: _____ Date: _____

Sprinkle of the Day: _____

Sprinkle Affirmation: _____

_____

_____

1. Today I am grateful for: _____

_____

_____

2. My intention for today is: _____

_____

_____

3. A challenge I might face today and how I will approach it:

_____

_____

4. One thought or belief I'm letting go of today is:

_____

_____

5. One thing I will do today to bring joy into my life is:

_____

_____

Sprinkle Reflection:

_____

_____

_____

_____

_____

_____

_____

_____

_____

_____

_____

_____

_____

_____

_____

_____

_____

_____

_____

_____

Day: _____ Date: _____

Sprinkle of the Day: _____

Sprinkle Affirmation: _____

_____

_____

1. Today I am grateful for: _____

_____

_____

2. My intention for today is: _____

_____

_____

3. A challenge I might face today and how I will approach it:

_____

_____

4. One thought or belief I'm letting go of today is:

_____

_____

5. One thing I will do today to bring joy into my life is:

_____

_____

Sprinkle Reflection:

_____

_____

_____

_____

_____

_____

_____

_____

_____

_____

_____

_____

_____

_____

_____

_____

_____

_____

_____

Day: _____ Date: _____

Sprinkle of the Day: _____

Sprinkle Affirmation: _____

_____

_____

1. Today I am grateful for: _____

_____

_____

2. My intention for today is: _____

_____

_____

3. A challenge I might face today and how I will approach it:

_____

_____

4. One thought or belief I'm letting go of today is:

_____

_____

5. One thing I will do today to bring joy into my life is:

_____

_____

Sprinkle Reflection:

_____

_____

_____

_____

_____

_____

_____

_____

_____

_____

_____

_____

_____

_____

_____

_____

_____

_____

_____

Day: _____ Date: _____

Sprinkle of the Day: _____

Sprinkle Affirmation: _____

_____

_____

1. Today I am grateful for: _____

_____

_____

2. My intention for today is: _____

_____

_____

3. A challenge I might face today and how I will approach it:

_____

_____

4. One thought or belief I'm letting go of today is:

_____

_____

5. One thing I will do today to bring joy into my life is:

_____

_____

Sprinkle Reflection:

_____

_____

_____

_____

_____

_____

_____

_____

_____

_____

_____

_____

_____

_____

_____

_____

_____

_____

_____

_____

Day: _____ Date: _____

Sprinkle of the Day: _____

Sprinkle Affirmation: _____

_____

_____

1. Today I am grateful for: _____

_____

_____

2. My intention for today is: _____

_____

_____

3. A challenge I might face today and how I will approach it:

_____

_____

4. One thought or belief I'm letting go of today is:

_____

_____

5. One thing I will do today to bring joy into my life is:

_____

_____

Sprinkle Reflection:

_____

_____

_____

_____

_____

_____

_____

_____

_____

_____

_____

_____

_____

_____

_____

_____

_____

_____

_____

Day: _____ Date: _____

Sprinkle of the Day: _____

Sprinkle Affirmation: _____

_____

_____

1. Today I am grateful for: _____

_____

_____

2. My intention for today is: _____

_____

_____

3. A challenge I might face today and how I will approach it:

_____

_____

4. One thought or belief I'm letting go of today is:

_____

_____

5. One thing I will do today to bring joy into my life is:

_____

_____

Sprinkle Reflection:

_____

_____

_____

_____

_____

_____

_____

_____

_____

_____

_____

_____

_____

_____

_____

_____

_____

_____

_____

_____

_____

Day: _____ Date: _____

Sprinkle of the Day: _____

Sprinkle Affirmation: _____

_____

_____

1. Today I am grateful for: _____

_____

_____

2. My intention for today is: _____

_____

_____

3. A challenge I might face today and how I will approach it:

_____

_____

4. One thought or belief I'm letting go of today is:

_____

_____

5. One thing I will do today to bring joy into my life is:

_____

_____

Sprinkle Reflection:

_____

_____

_____

_____

_____

_____

_____

_____

_____

_____

_____

_____

_____

_____

_____

_____

_____

_____

_____

_____

_____

Day: _____ Date: _____

Sprinkle of the Day: _____

Sprinkle Affirmation: _____

_____

_____

1. Today I am grateful for: _____

_____

_____

2. My intention for today is: _____

_____

_____

3. A challenge I might face today and how I will approach it:

_____

_____

4. One thought or belief I'm letting go of today is:

_____

_____

5. One thing I will do today to bring joy into my life is:

_____

_____

Sprinkle Reflection:

_____

_____

_____

_____

_____

_____

_____

_____

_____

_____

_____

_____

_____

_____

_____

_____

_____

_____

Day: _____ Date: _____

Sprinkle of the Day: _____

Sprinkle Affirmation: _____

_____

_____

1. Today I am grateful for: _____

_____

_____

2. My intention for today is: _____

_____

_____

3. A challenge I might face today and how I will approach it:

_____

_____

4. One thought or belief I'm letting go of today is:

_____

_____

5. One thing I will do today to bring joy into my life is:

_____

_____

Sprinkle Reflection:

_____

_____

_____

_____

_____

_____

_____

_____

_____

_____

_____

_____

_____

_____

_____

_____

_____

_____

_____

Day: _____ Date: _____

Sprinkle of the Day: _____

Sprinkle Affirmation: _____

_____

_____

1. Today I am grateful for: _____

_____

_____

2. My intention for today is: _____

_____

_____

3. A challenge I might face today and how I will approach it:

_____

_____

4. One thought or belief I'm letting go of today is:

_____

_____

5. One thing I will do today to bring joy into my life is:

_____

_____

Sprinkle Reflection:

_____

_____

_____

_____

_____

_____

_____

_____

_____

_____

_____

_____

_____

_____

_____

_____

_____

_____

_____

_____

_____

Day: _____ Date: _____

Sprinkle of the Day: _____

Sprinkle Affirmation: _____

_____

_____

1. Today I am grateful for: _____

_____

_____

2. My intention for today is: _____

_____

_____

3. A challenge I might face today and how I will approach it:

_____

_____

4. One thought or belief I'm letting go of today is:

_____

_____

5. One thing I will do today to bring joy into my life is:

_____

_____

Sprinkle Reflection:

_____

_____

_____

_____

_____

_____

_____

_____

_____

_____

_____

_____

_____

_____

_____

_____

_____

_____

_____

_____

_____

Day: _____ Date: _____

Sprinkle of the Day: _____

Sprinkle Affirmation: _____

_____

_____

1. Today I am grateful for: _____

_____

_____

2. My intention for today is: _____

_____

_____

3. A challenge I might face today and how I will approach it:

_____

_____

4. One thought or belief I'm letting go of today is:

_____

_____

5. One thing I will do today to bring joy into my life is:

_____

_____

Sprinkle Reflection:

_____

_____

_____

_____

_____

_____

_____

_____

_____

_____

_____

_____

_____

_____

_____

_____

_____

_____

_____

_____

Day: _____ Date: _____

Sprinkle of the Day: _____

Sprinkle Affirmation: _____

_____

_____

1. Today I am grateful for: _____

_____

_____

2. My intention for today is: _____

_____

_____

3. A challenge I might face today and how I will approach it:

_____

_____

4. One thought or belief I'm letting go of today is:

_____

_____

5. One thing I will do today to bring joy into my life is:

_____

_____

Sprinkle Reflection:

_____

_____

_____

_____

_____

_____

_____

_____

_____

_____

_____

_____

_____

_____

_____

_____

_____

_____

_____

_____

_____

Day: _____ Date: _____

Sprinkle of the Day: _____

Sprinkle Affirmation: _____

_____

_____

1. Today I am grateful for: _____

_____

_____

2. My intention for today is: _____

_____

_____

3. A challenge I might face today and how I will approach it:

_____

_____

4. One thought or belief I'm letting go of today is:

_____

_____

5. One thing I will do today to bring joy into my life is:

_____

_____

Sprinkle Reflection:

_____

_____

_____

_____

_____

_____

_____

_____

_____

_____

_____

_____

_____

_____

_____

_____

_____

_____

_____

Day: _____ Date: _____

Sprinkle of the Day: _____

Sprinkle Affirmation: _____

_____

_____

1. Today I am grateful for: _____

_____

_____

2. My intention for today is: _____

_____

_____

3. A challenge I might face today and how I will approach it:

_____

_____

4. One thought or belief I'm letting go of today is:

_____

_____

5. One thing I will do today to bring joy into my life is:

_____

_____

Sprinkle Reflection:

_____

_____

_____

_____

_____

_____

_____

_____

_____

_____

_____

_____

_____

_____

_____

_____

_____

_____

_____

_____

www.ingramcontent.com/pod-product-compliance
Lightning Source LLC
Chambersburg PA
CBHW050441150626
46551CB00028B/977